Scorpio Man...

No One Likes Romeo

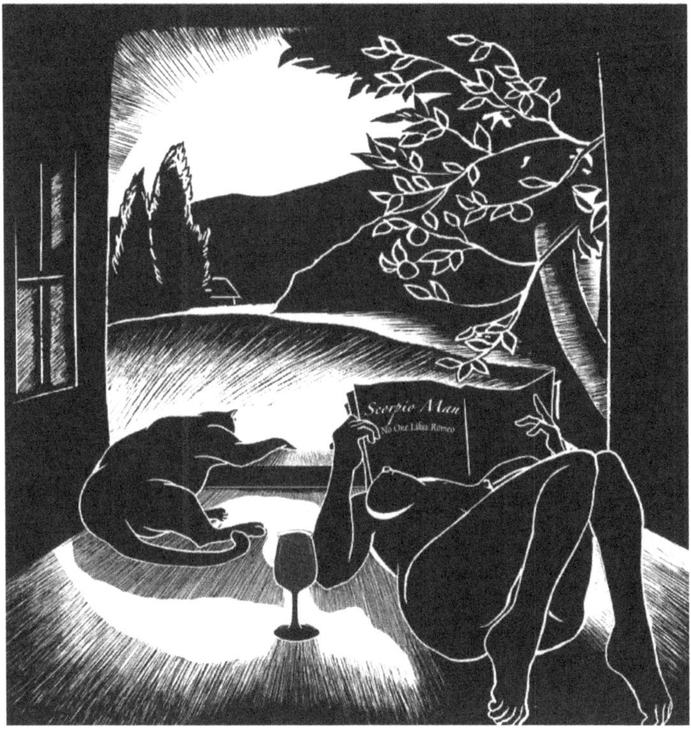

Love, Lust and Limerence

Disclaimer

Scorpio Man… No One Likes Romeo

Love, Lust and Limerence

Printed by Ingram Spark

Printed in the United States of America

Available from Website and other retail outlets

First Printing Edition, 2022

ISBN 13 979-8-9872964-0-0

DEDICATION

This book is dedicated to all the poetry aficionados in the world who still believe in love without judgment and expectations. My writing is devoted to those people who unapologetically crave intimacy in their lives. If you have read this book and find the content valuable, then I ask you to contribute what you think that value is worth. Do not hesitate to donate as much as you wish or can afford at this time. Your donations help with covering my expenses, time, knowledge, and my ability to create more stories like those that you have enjoyed. Thank you and feel free to share your comments!

PayPal QR code:

Cash App QR code:

Venmo QR code:

TABLE OF CONTENTS

Symbol Meanings

COM – Companion • LUS – Lust • LOV – Love
FET – Fetish • EMO – Emotional • TSB – Testimonial

	Chapter Titles	**Symbol**
	Preface	COM
1	Mr. Temporary	LUS
2	The Scorpio Man	LOV
3	Esoteric Tongue	EMO
4	Tunisian Flower	LUS
5	She May Drive You Nuts	LOV
6	Pepper	FET
7	What's for Breakfast?	LUS
8	Wandering Eyes	LUS
9	Lust Odyssey	LUS
10	Love Me Hate Me	LOV
11	Resistless	LUS
12	The Big O	EMO
13	What League?	LUS
14	Why Not?	LUS
15	Red Aura	EMO
16	Primal Instincts	LUS

	Chapter Titles	**Symbol**
17	Peaches and Cream	LUS
18	Can You Keep a Secret?	LUS
19	Black Licorice	FET
20	Forbidden Fruit	LUS
21	Principles of Economics	LUS
22	Sapiosexuals	COM
23	Hello Kitty	LUS
24	Invisible Chains	LOV
25	Knocking at the Wrong Door	EMO
26	My House	EMO
27	Baritone Pheromones	TSB
28	Computer Luv	LUS
29	Fisherman's Virtue	TSB
30	The Thrilla in Vanilla	LOV
31	The Night Shift	LUS
32	5:55 AM	EMP
33	Zodiac Signs	COM

PREFACE

I wrote this collection of poems with the intention of letting go of all expectations so that I may grow and take the journey on a path to heal and finally love myself. Scorpio Man's Nobody Likes Romeo is a poetic portrayal of a conflicted man who is perfectly composed on his surface. Wickedly intellectual, financially successful, powerful and respected, he has an uncanny ability to attract women, especially those who tend to only see as far as his initial presentation. But deep beneath his surface, he is a man pulled in many directions, lost in lechery, limerence, temptation; filled with fleeting desires and fearing commitment.

This offering is a self-reflection of a man both predator and prey. And as the author, I am hoping that perhaps my remorse for my impulsive adventures might diminish as I purge these wild, sensual and sometimes savage experiences.

In Nobody Likes Romeo, I take you, the reader, with me to the secret inner world of Scorpio Man. I lay bare my life and thoughts as a troubled ego trembling on the inner surface of my existence. The narrative of my mysteriously aloof nature coupled with my ability to charm and flatter will fill you with chills, eroticism and even revulsion.

If one young susceptible man or woman can be prevented from traveling too far down the same tricky and potentially painful path, the regret I have experienced and my ensuing uncomfortable evolution will be worth it.

This collection of poems serves as the precursor for my upcoming book

Scorpio Man... The Professor's Memoirs.

Scorpio Man...
No One Likes Romeo

Love, Lust and Limerence

Mr. Temporary

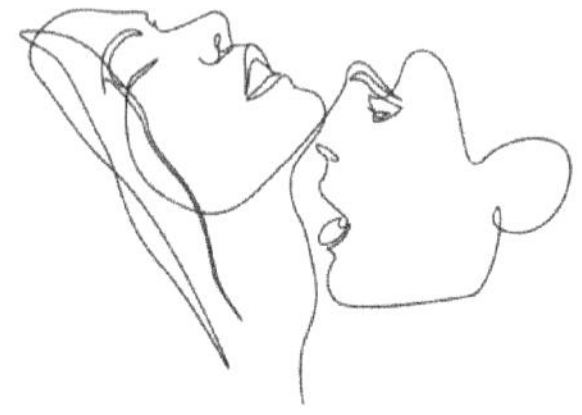

In and out, in and out I thrust
Your legs wrapped tightly around my waist
Your arms draped over my back in and out I clutch, you adjust...
our moans fill up the space

Out and in, out and in... I thrust
Your fingernails dig deep into my skin
Carving Tic Tac Toe, while my teeth clench your neckline as my
hard steel plated missile penetrates your crust

For I am not a one night stand, I am a man
A master of pleasure that can perform to any mood or measure,
any temperature in any weather, any dimension, any condition or
any span

I'll listen to your problems, I might not solve them
But I can give you something to get your mind right off them
Don't worry about your girlfriends
Babe we lost them
Searching for Superman but he don't fly around often

Instead of looking at your watch
Let us toast with some shots
"Bartender, can we get another vodka on the rocks?"

Cuz right now I have a clear view of the perfect rearview

With melons so exquisite they should put it on a menu

I vividly remember how you looked in those jeans that night had
me feeling some type of way
And I just want to say
I loved the way they grip your assets, every curve every crevice
Pulled perfectly between your cheeks, as your hips move and
sway

So succumb to your needs and be fulfilled with slow deep strokes
of my long hard happy stick ...

I kiss your lips softly twisting your nipples as they poke, eye
contact

Gazing deep within your soul to find out exactly how you tick

But I will only give you part of your wish as I pull out only to
tease you with the tip
Over and over... driving you crazy, driving you to your edge
"Please babe I need it ..."drive it deep in me please"... as you beg
to take another trip

The Scorpio Man

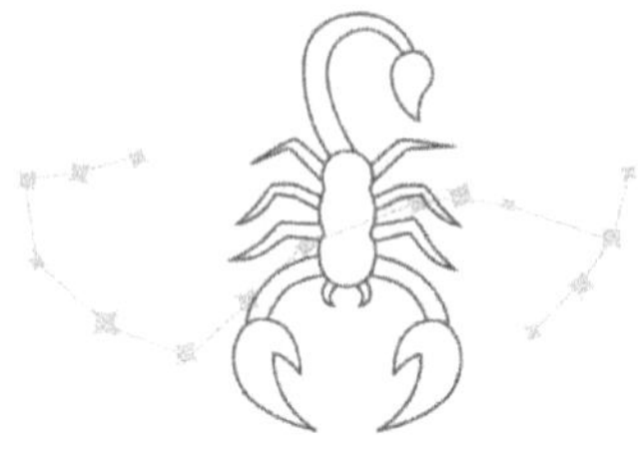

From the shoes to the socks
He's a walking paradox
But in the eyes of a wolf or a fox
All they see is lamb chops

That's the allure...
He may seem obscure
But know he's highly aware
The perfect combination of truth and dare
Mixed signals from his stare
Willing to call the bluff of anyone disguised as tough and
unsure...

For he is … a gentleman of leisure
Dressed to impress but his physical appeal does not reflect what is
real
It is only an illusion
Pay attention to the mannerisms which lead to confusion

A man of mystery a modern day enigma
With a boyish face, charm and exquisite taste
Captivating with a hidden agenda

"I desire" is his motto
In all black, head to toe like a desperado
Silhouette with a red aura, outlining his fedora
While sipping Remy or Moscato

His life is like a real life soap opera
Full of passion, pursuits and romantic commutes

Ruled by his root chakra

He's a rolling stone, a digital nomad
For he's either all in or not at all
A water sign defined with a push-pull persona
Maybe the greatest or the worst lover you've ever had

For on a good day he's brash
On a bad day he'll clash
Any ill intent he may cache
Forgiving but never forgetting
But be wary of his sting
If you intervene with his esteem
It'll be camouflaged with a laugh

Esoteric Tongue

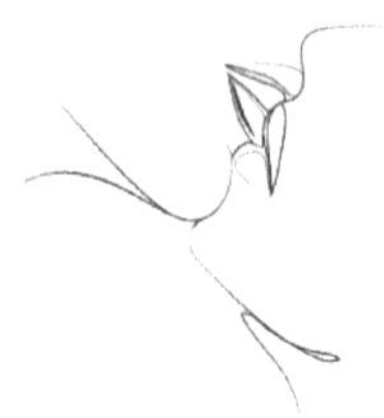

Each and every experience is different
Transparency in each moment even with the same partner,
separated by time and space, set apart by a unique place called
"satisfactory" often overlooked by the ignorant

The thrill, the rush
The touch from my fingertips while whispering sweet nothings in
your ear
Justify your cheeks to blush

Every woman is mystery waiting to be solved
The secrecy of when the hue of her skin flushes the color of rose
petals, it's a sign to get involved

So I move in close with intensity
My words, your brain, your heart share the same sensitivity
To be loved brings out a distinct humility
No fear, no anger, no danger just to be
Captured and suspended in infinite invincibility

I'm imagining you want to kiss me...
Never batting a lash although my intent is somewhat risky
Though I'm not a mind reader, I'm a mind feeder...
Food for thought like peaches and cream topped with pralines as
sweet as Tennessee whiskey

I vowed.. never surrender to the momentum of mediocrity
My passion and pain guides me through the dichotomy in a
universe of diverse biology

No matter how much we tried
Our feelings cannot be denied
As we are tied, bonded like atoms
Hard to fathom the connection to my madam
Somehow survived

Far from perfect
My presence brings her inner emotions to the surface
Offering her the closest thing to experiencing God, the closest
thing to fulfilling our purpose

From scratch
We start again, with confusion and delusions
Thirsty for a transfusion to breathe life back into a stagnant
predicament
A tale of lost innocence starving for solutions

Tunisian Flower

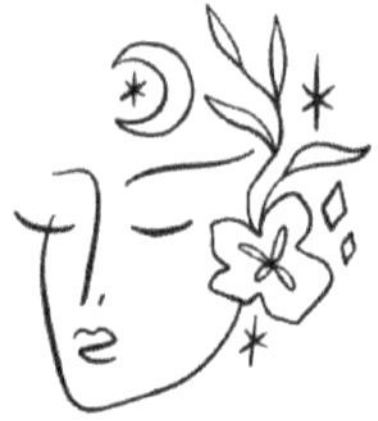

They kiss one final time before saying their last goodbyes
Her eyes, filled with tears of sadness, he wipes the tears from her
cheeks and pulls her in close…
"I'll see you soon" he says, but it's all lies

"December!" she says in a stern voice "I'll see you in December…
"promise me..."

"I promise," he says... Knowing he will probably never see her
again
He lied because he didn't want to push the dagger in her heart any
deeper than it's already been

Under the Tunisian sun, mid-July, seven days of pleasure, passion
and empty promises was overwhelming for her
But for him it was a recurrence
To live, lust and move on providing false reassurance

For he never set out to break any young girl's heart
But he's never been one to play by the rules
He's a slave to pleasure, lost innocence
Claiming victims cast out in the name of love in a sea of
misguided fools.

From California to Tokyo, he's a modern-day Pinocchio
What a beautiful liar to set her heart on fire here's Romeo... and
no one likes Romeo

She may drive you nuts

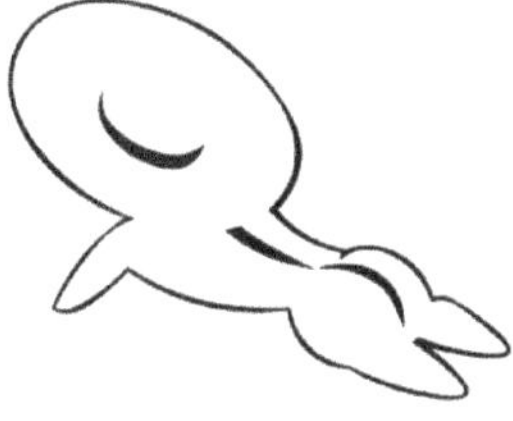

Those sultry eyes, her laugh makes me smile
And proud to be a man where you can spot it from a mile

Maybe she's been hurt before... so have I
To the point the pain drove me to where I felt I should never try

Fear...inside I've cried many times but my masculinity would
never let my eyes drop a single tear
Though I've never been a penitent man sometimes I crave
watching the waves crash from the pier

I wonder if she ever thinks about me...probably not
Because if she did I wouldn't have to wonder and I would've
already had a shot
Or maybe I live in a place where God must've forgot
And the plot is to figure out how to evolve into the perfect key to
pick her mystery lock

In time...it seems time is never on my side
when it comes to who I want vs who I deserve, then there's pride
which makes limerence worth the ride

Maybe I'm just naive, conflicted since a seed, ignoring all the
signs that I refuse to receive

I came to her as a helpless romantic, a half-completed canvas
To where she drew everywhere except the finishing strokes of her
brush down my yellow brick road which makes me nuts now, I
can't return to Kansas

Each vibration I send with no hesitation seems like a rejection
Then I'm back full circle to where my emotions penetrate my
skull like an injection

The truth is... I do think of her often...
So often I can't separate lust from impulse as I'm ignorant to
precaution

I want her to know chivalry isn't dead
It just hasn't been fed, but the appetite is led by the thoughts in my
head

I can't speak for all men, but I do sympathize
with all the conflicted souls that covet a real woman in hope for
better lives

Pepper

Pepper will make you act right...

All the naughty girls in the world
Flirting with temptation
Unknowingly covet this taboo stimulation

Where the blind leads the blind
The so called innocent gets taken from behind
Right now is not the time for a sixty nine
Every beautiful bubble butt gets desired but ends up
Getting propped up and spread wide
Ready to be aligned...

Pepper will make you act right...

Dressed head to toe in black leather
Every masochist's dream
Willing to make her mark
Red... increasing the blood flow that creates a sensitive glow
from unexpected moans and screams

Pepper will make you act right...

Back and forth she sways
Ready to strike when you don't obey
Your anticipation is burning
Bracing for the moment... a delay
This type of foreplay takes all your worries away

Pepper will make you act right...

First we use a feather
Gentle strokes of the skin to blend
Every absorbing touch makes everything feel better

In contrast...
Any opportunity she gets to strike that juicy ass
Pleasure takes control therefore she cannot pass

Pepper will make you act right...

And if you refuse to play by these rules
Then leave... as you are now excused

But if you take a chance in this forbidden romance
There are three rules you must consent to in advance:

Rule # 1
You must consent
Peppers' intent is evident
Good dick is not a right it's a privilege... a bona-fide benefit
That area between the bottom of your cheeks and the top of your
thigh, leaves every submissive high and decadent

Rule # 2
Leave all rebellion at the door
If you can slow down and breathe
Be ready to receive
Then you will be begging for more
The fine line between pain and pleasure
Is a hidden treasure...
Vanilla acts don't have a place in this space
When Pepper is in charge of applying pressure

Rule # 3
Last but not least
If you're looking for something gentle
You won't find it here, as tonight we switch gears
Pepper gets you wetter as she awakens the beast

So grip the sheets, and let it all out
Pepper goes to work overtime
Until you call out her name...then the game will cease

Pepper will make you act right...

What's for breakfast?

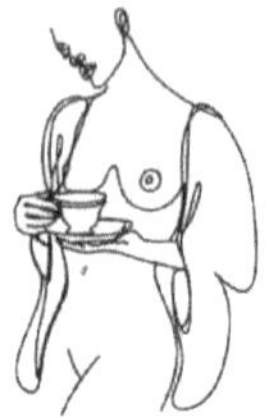

You lie still on your back while your breasts rest motionless, my
mind roves
Perfect like two eggs over easy slightly charred coming right off
the stove
Your lower half is covered in linen white, oh what a sight,
thoughts of last night was another height, lo and behold

Too early for the hors d'oeuvres, as my voyeur tendencies cannot
be contained
Because what we're about to cook up in this kitchen doesn't have
to be explained

As you flip on your side your buns golden and bronzed from the
sun appear as if they came right out of the oven
My mouth watering as they look amazingly edible as the coconut
oil resembles butter spread all over a muffin

My bacon is hard and crispy just the way you like it
Despite it lying on a rectangular shape plate my intent is to tease
your appetite then spike it

For we have the right to entice with plenty on this buffet
Let's take it slow or we can play the rough way
Lay you down like blueberry pancakes, enact like flapjacks
smothered in maple syrup with a touch of whip cream
complimented with the right amount of extreme to cause a flood
way

Your fruit is so ripe so juicy and sweet
The echoes from your moans, the mattress squeaks, to the same
rhythm, the same beat, as we thrust in lust.. balls deep, until we
pass right out to sleep

So when we awake, let's create a shake
Mix up the finest ingredients
As you milk me of my deviance

And if making brunch is a crime, I'll admit my guilt and proudly
do the time
So when I'm released, we will feast
And wash it down with a bottle of love potion number nine...

Wandering Eyes

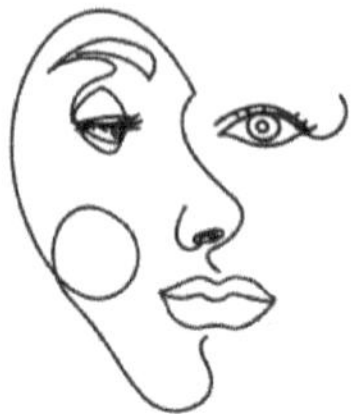

My wandering eyes got me in trouble, yes I admit I fucked up
Lucked up with the 20 year old vixen most men would label stuck up

I've peeped her for a while now, mannerisms, her moves, her attitude
But for some reason she gives me special attention in my time of need
For that I give her gratitude

How did I get here I ask myself
Infatuation and lust are ultimately bad for my health

But for me that's how it starts
It doesn't come from the heart
It comes from what I'm told is the dark
However the "it" stimulates my entire existence which flames my spark

Monogamy for years I tried, petrified each time I've gazed into your eyes and lied

To my core this is not who I am, my character is not a sham
But how do I explain myself and not come across as selfish like I don't give a damn

Is there one woman out there that can satisfy my ever sexual need?
Someone who can feed the beast inside when I can't fight the urge of greed

Each time I spread my seed knowing it's happily received
In the right space and time the right partner that will readily
conceive

Maybe my delusions have taken their toll
It never gets old
My quest for perfection, my misdirection and attempts for
providing protection have become nothing more than
manipulative ways for me to keep control

The Controller he moves from a place of fear
When he's afraid he strikes with no plan, all sheer with intents
only to be severe

My apologies, I've given you a false sense of hope
I was taught anything worth having takes work
However my sins don't comprehend accountability and any
thoughts to elope

Lust Odyssey

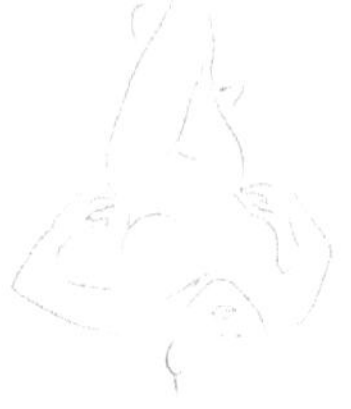

Hello again...our last encounter must have not been disappointing
I aim to please, whenever you're in the mood so here I am, would
you care about joining

I don't want to waste a moment not even a single breath
And if this is our last time I'm going to treat it as if it's my first,
fucking each other until death

I admit sometimes my Scorpio ways get the best of me
Without them I wouldn't have been able to live out every fantasy
or destiny

I love that. you put up with my kinky tendencies
In fact... I think you like them just as much as me to where we
match the same energies

So skip the foreplay for now and let's get straight to it
But keep on the blindfold because I lust the body language you're
giving off
I understand because I speak it fluid

So take a deep breath, exhale away all your worry
Troubles don't live here, so you're safe no need to be in a hurry

Every kiss every touch every squeeze every moan
Every pressure point responds to my rhythm as if we are moving
in sync to a metronome
Every erogenous zone is momentarily my home as I improvise to
give you crimson eyes as we explore the unknown

Love me Hate me

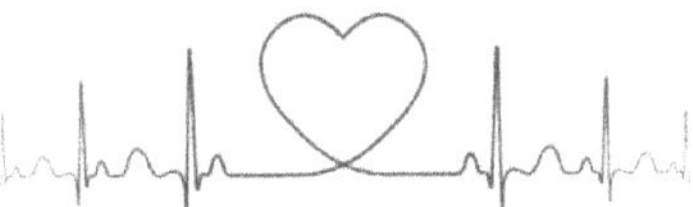

You love me you hate me
You love me you hate me
You love me you hate me
then hate me some more

You love me you hate me
You love me you hate me
You love me you hate me
then hate me for what they love me for

Headaches and heartbreaks
Making the same mistakes
Right place wrong time
I want it if just a taste
I'd rather be face to face
To see you with an embrace
Not interested in the chase
I'm interested in the space

First the day comes and then night falls
Nocturnal… you only see me when the night calls
You want to make love in the tub then you
might call
But when you like it rough I'm the one to make your tights fall

Manipulative lies become disguised in smiles or help
Until you look in the mirror and realize you're lying to yourself

Everything I see is a reflection of me
So why are you fucking with me
You must want something from me

When the vibration halts our rhythm becomes invert, as hurt
people hurt
The face exerts the universal language without a single blurt

My honesty, I feel honestly scares you away
And whenever I edit myself without speaking my truth I tend to
have a shitty day

Hot and cold, cold and hot
When the feelings are lukewarm
My emotions will boycott

You want my good but not my bad
But my bad is all I had when my good wasn't enough, it made me
tough, when I was sad

Let's finish this chapter, turn the page
Light the sage and keep it burning
Redefine our means of association
Pleasure and pain as the world keeps turning

For we are lovers not fighters, kissers and biters
How about we pull another all nighter
Then set the mattress on fire

Resistless

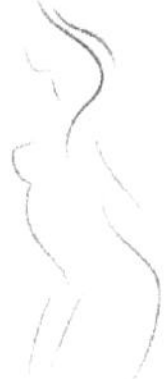

Kiss them lick them suck them pluck them
Make them wet and hard filled up from the blood rush
I cuff with both hands as I sit on your chest so I can fuck them

When I circle with the tip of my tongue tell me babe do you like
that?
Gripping them tight like a sponge while your moans let out a
slight humm… biting your lower lip, tell me baby can you psych
that?

Each and every time you're with me you have to give up control
And each and every time that saying will never get old

So let's pull out the blindfold, strap you nicely to the bed
Wrist by wrist, arm by arm spread wide in each direction as you
await to be led

I want a piece of your soul, not all just a fraction
A big piece of your forbidden fruit without interference or
distraction

So before we adios.... I conjure rosebud bitter dose...let the sillage
leave you froze from my bottom notes
Take one whiff... my ardor will leave you comatose

The Big O

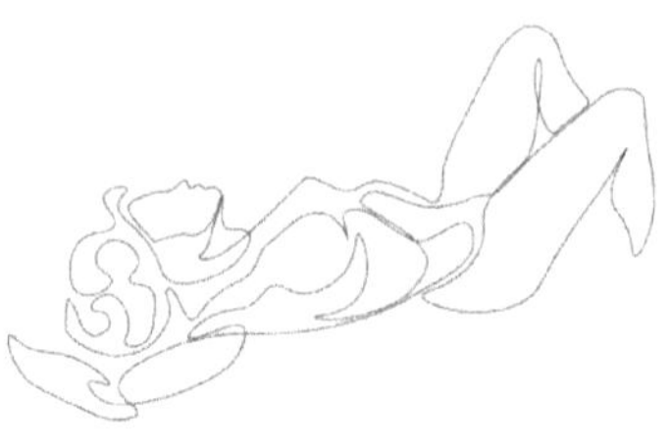

Do you remember the first time?
The feeling, the mood, the sensation
Where you felt excited, blissed out like a celebration which
ultimately blew your mind

The first sign of puberty which paves the path to maturity
Whenever the world seems cold you can isolate and lock yourself
away to indulge in your own pleasure security

Those memories that unlocked the secrets to Pandora's box often
gave you a rush
Other times made you ashamed
You would satiate away the hate and disgust
To alleviate away in hush

Your crush, your fantasy, your exhibitions of risqué explorations
Declarations of your own independence, dependent only upon
your salacious observations

When the blood left your brain and feet
Causing your nature to steep
At that moment you reached out to make the connection
No rejections, just reflections in images of perfection eventually
lead to the most soul satisfying ejection

Self pleasure of any measure in discreet, will in brief, eventually
deliver relief...
So paint your canvas, as beautiful, as deep as you get lost like the
city of Atlantis
Exploring your own Utopian paradise as your fantasies become
motif

What League?

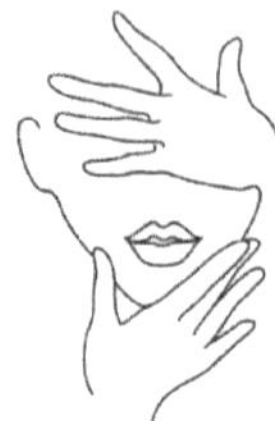

My father said "act your wage not your age"
But I say why should it matter
if we're on the same page and not the same rage, people always
commit to chatter

The sweetest taboo I'm giving you
Makes you think deeply about the risk
Reluctance and curiosity just don't mix
Although a part of your desire is to have a taste of the bisque

I'm the love from below, the thunder from down under...the one
you think about with your man and makes you wonder about this
long anaconda

I don't need to text your number no need for hesitation
Just look deep within me and prep for mental stimulation
Let me lead you with a kiss
Are you afraid of sensation?
Just be patient...aware and anticipating ...
No need to feel judged no need to keep us waiting

Appearances, differences lead to once in a lifetime deliverances
When was the last time you had an experience that changed the
way you view distances?

Why Not?

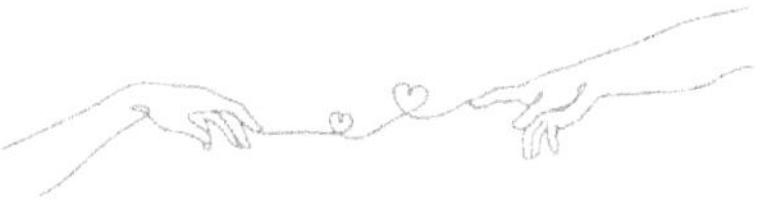

I remember hearing my name screamed in her shattering orgasms.
oh god. oh god. oh fuck.
Is god fuck?
Am i god?
Am i fuck?
I clasp your fingers into my tight fists as I pin them behind your head.
You didn't mind begging as my soft primal recipient as your body responds with wetness and small whimpering moans sailing through your emotional whirlwind.
Free your mind...mouth wet and skin tissue thin, hips lifting to meet mine.
Why beg to me to bite more and push your edge further. More...?
Pause. Look into my eyes, she says.
"I will never belong to you. I have always wanted more than a good girl should
but I will share this moment with you and I will let you break me open to the great beyond and the source of all things."
"I am never happier than when I lose consciousness of my smaller self and merge orgiastically with all that is pulsating in the abyss."
Dark matter + White light = synced trust
The whole universe is fucking itself.
So why not us?

Red Aura

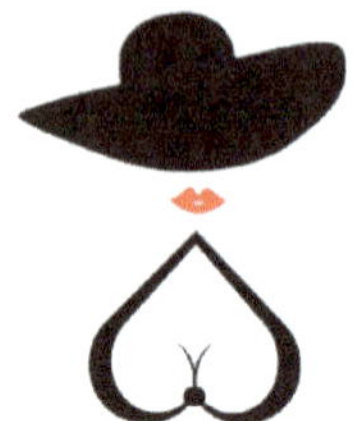

Mmmm....those red pumps... my heartbeat jumps... as your high heels stalk
Click clack on the pavement
Chin high as you walk
If walls could talk that matching tight red dress wouldn't balk
Sex appeal, glamour galore...killing me softly leaving a trail of victims outlined in chalk

Cherry red lipstick highlights your lips
Lunar Lady answering the call of the wild during a blood moon eclipse

There's a natural mystic which flows specific
Deeply rooted as far as the Pacific in which stirs up something voyeuristic
locked in a trance with visions of you in a forbidden dance
that defies the laws of physics

Bittersweet and unique sometimes cold as ice but often hot like red lava
Sometimes ferocious, her dosha's more pitta than vata

Ignoring all red flags while sipping an Argentine Malbec from the finest red grapes
Integrate faith and prophecy then there's no debate
Only hate from envy that cannot relate
Therefore we dine like kings and queens then indulge on red velvet cake

Went from pigtails and French barrettes

To cigarettes and now an amazing silhouette hopping out of little
red corvettes
Strawberry letter twenty four I dedicate with room for more
To the one I can never forget

25% black and 25% white equals 1 shade of gray
With 49 in disarray
The missing ingredient hidden or even forbidden from the
spectrum is vivid
As the dusk of the sun gloaming during the highlight of a twilight
after the sunset day

Love, lust and limerence
Intensity, spontaneous and passionate relationships
What color like no other symbolizes affection?
So bright that it exudes the right perception of perfection

Primal Instincts

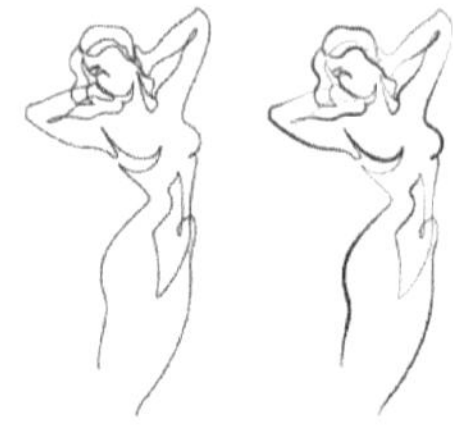

I am an animal, primal without a doubt
For everyday I stalk my prey, prowling throughout my routes

My intentions are felt and understood
I can adapt to any mood, any style
As any apex would

The things I'm going to do to you, you probably wouldn't approve
But if you trust that my intentions are never to hurt you but only
to move...
your mind, body and spirit in search for the rhythmic groove

I do not believe that eyes are the gateway to the soul but one of
many
For that I find serenity in my vicinity
To confide an interconnection as we both pay tribute that's worth
every penny

My resonance strikes a chord releasing the perfect melody
I watch anticipating the right time to devour you oh so gently
The suspense is tense...leaving your peers in jealousy and envy

I put it all on the line it fuels the passion
I'm possessed
Like a wild jackal obsessed
Whenever I'm in the mood for flesh

I grab, you gasp...
Out into the wild as my fingers clasped
Your throat, I squeeze, you choke

I please, with ease I let go
Even though your eyes say no
Your panties are saturated and soaked

So as my victim should lay
With no escape nor stray
I leave you breathless with more than you could take or say
Until finally you surrender proudly as my slay

The prowl feeds the growl in which the style breeds the vowel
A.E.I.O.U.
The choice of being eaten alive like a feline on a pursue

Peaches and Cream

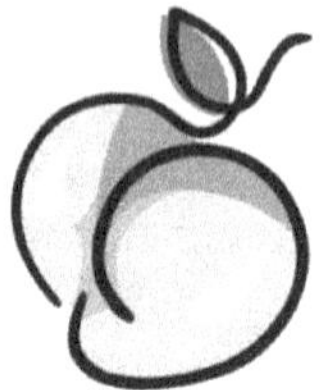

After playing hard to get for so long, you are now a lifetime
prisoner in my fantasy
You are sentenced to seduction for being the object of my desire
As reality hits you're now ineligible for amnesty

As I'm thinking about your punishment I set the mood and adjust
your settings
All I can imagine is your delicious ass trapped in those skin tight
black leggings

So what do you think of me wanting to bend you over in those
leggings and tease your sexy ass for a few ticks then bite a huge
hole
As I bite wide my tongue escapes through and barely teases my
mark, startled...
Makes you jump, giving me the sign of who is in control

I then rip through the spandex with my teeth
Leaving just enough room to lather your
creamy pink slit with my ambitious tongue rhythmically teasing
your sheath

You can't stand it as I'm driving you crazy..."oh babe, you're
driving me crazy with that tongue"
I know babe but... please be patient…
It's all part of the fun to get your head, mind and body sprung

The tip of my tongue travels back and forth between your
beautiful bottom and your tight pink kitty...
You urge me to stop but I won't as I bind you with my hands

Your bottom over my face to where you can't move and can only take it
As I continue to dish out over and over
Until you beg me...but my tongue has no pity

Can you keep a secret?

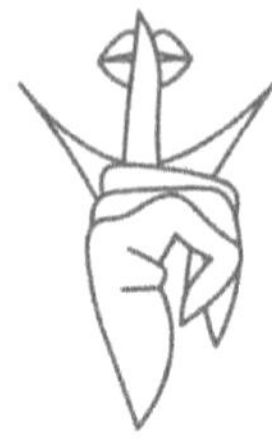

What's a promise if you can't keep it?
What's a secret?
If you can't see it, can you still believe it?
What would it take for you to achieve it?

It's the little things that I notice, those are the things that steer my
focus
I adjust my attitude I set the mood, I then spread you out like a
blue lotus

No I don't want to wait in vain
Take me to a place on a one way train
To where your love wave hits my brain like a main line injected
directly in my vein

I'm an addict, addicted to explicit and sensual thrills
I'm a masochist, infatuated with the cycles of pleasure and pain in
which it fulfills
the emptiness inside and gives me the chills

I'm here to guide you on a secret quest
The path leads to the valley of your love fest
Though I highly recommend the toxic sex
For that I am the best; here to fulfill any special request

What I desire doesn't require clothes or makeup
Just be bold and give up control
Let the feeling take hold
Then everything will be as easy as a layup

Black Licorice

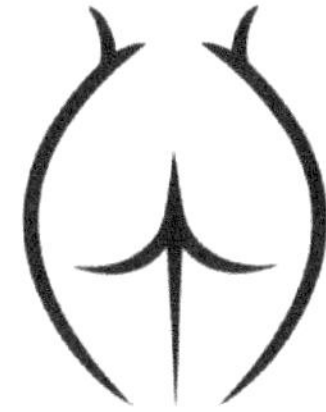

My thoughts are ecstatic my libido is electrified
By now you know my little secret so whenever you choose to
tempt me, my pupils dilate, my heart beats petrified

Seduce me in those pants, melt me with your lips
Mesmerize me with your walk
Hypnotize me with your hips

The way the smooth texture clings tight to your frame
Stretches over your luscious peaches absorbing everything to
claim
Your skintight silhouette on display has my hormones going
insane
You know you've got me hooked ever since the first look
Down to your matching boots, that racy bodysuit makes me crave
your passion fruit without any shame
You're my vision of Chris Isaac's depiction of Wicked Game ...

Oh vicious vixen, lady of the night, dressed in all black like a
pistol packing outlaw
Each time you walk by I want to grab a hold and bite, then pray to
God for lock jaw

Tush wrapped shiny and tight like the perfect gift under my
Christmas tree
But on display for all the voyeurs to see

I can sense your need to be desired, an object of affection because
your outfit garners attention
Deep down I know your intentions

The hyphephiliacs watch as you marvel in exhibition

Show me what you got without showing me
Let my imagination run wild with premonitions unknowingly
You're the image Santana had in mind when he stroked the cords
of his electric guitar with a light tap

Black magic woman here I am again caught in your Venus Flytrap

Forbidden Fruit

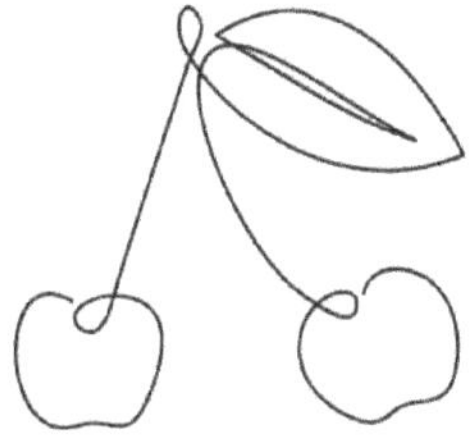

I will not eat of the forbidden fruit
Although it is very tempting I jeopardize robbing her of her youth
Her truth, yet she isn't aware, drawn in as I can see by the allure in her stare

She thinks she's ready but she's not even close
How could I even consider the idea, which could cost me my reputation, my career
The inclination forces me to stay on my toes

I will not eat of the forbidden fruit, for it is forbidden
The signs are not hidden and that ring on her finger says it was written
long before I came into the picture with charm to disarm that had her smitten

I refuse to eat of the forbidden fruit
Therefore I choose, I've paid my dues
My choices fulfill my faith and prophecy
To where I'm the only one who is stopping me
Therefore I choose principles and rules over illicit taboos

My grandmother gave me the best advice in the world
She said "don't entertain what you don't want"
Sometimes the thoughts haunt even though I get a thrill from the hunt
The best decision is to walk away and refrain nonchalant

So I will not eat of the forbidden fruit...
If my truth is not foreseen in the seed, the root or the pursuit

Principles of Economics

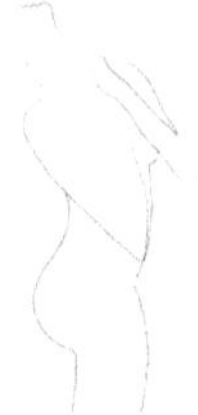

The more you demand the more I supply therefore I provide and
you abide
Together we decide
To meet at the equilibrium of lust or confide.. or… divide

What's love without lust, what's a relationship without trust,
what's sensation without stimulation nothing more than a
differential equation robust

Take away the sex, then what do we have
Let's do the math
one + one = two
Then what do we do if we can't see past the linear path

Dreams are for the gullible, how about we create something
untouchable
Instead of something unlovable or destructible
Let's explore into an abyss of rainbows so colorful...
We replicate intimacy mixing the sun and the moon into infinite
multiples

Cuz back in the day, women would hold out until they got a ring
Or the wedding of their dreams
Well time flies, oh what a lullaby, look at the opportunity costs of
how ego lost our queens

With a shortage of desirable men, market efficiency has decreased
Facing a shortage and a mortgage the women have settled for the
beast

Could I sell you on something reciprocal instead of typical?
Rather than inferior, something mythical?
Do you believe in miracles?
Or how about pinnacles?
If love is economics, then, how do you feel about principles?

Sapiosexuals

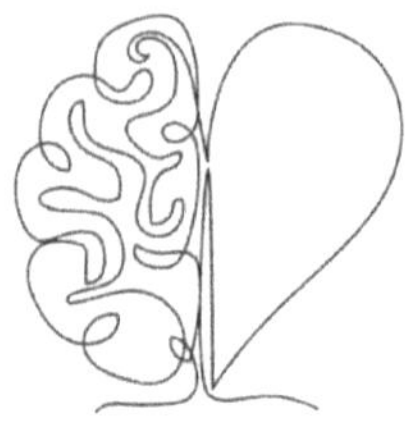

Before words there are thoughts
The art of thinking before speaking
A reason... the definition of meaning
Stimulation refined by the word...intriguing

My eye contact validates in good faith
Anticipating that my intentions are not a mistake
So when my heart beat gyrates
We ascend no longer as primates
In conjunction we vibrate...

The appreciation of deep conversations moved her to a place she
found solace
Craving language abstruse to a novice
The dialect of a God and Goddess
Relatable only to a Laureate or Colossus

Only the experienced, well traveled or the imaginative
Can give her the fondness of affection where
Intellects crave a place only love lives
To where words and syllables appear invisible to the naked eye
Undescribed by any adjective

The brain maintains as the most vital organ
Verbal intercourse of racy subjects, as vivid as any description of
a dire prescription
Only Doctor Feelgood knows the right proportion

To align with a lover by design
Leaving the shallow to hide behind its shadow
In pursuits to be declined

Not worthy of exchanging knowledge and philosophical beliefs
Which gratifies an imminent release
The search for inner peace in an object of affection stirred in the
right direction
Disciplined by immortal techniques

Word of the wise, those that despise shallow identities
Take pleasure in finding pleasure in electromagnetic energies
Her pineal stimulates when she absorbs organic chemistry
Beauty, booty and brains engineering the symmetrical balance of
rhythm and talents
Effort and consistency

Hello Kitty

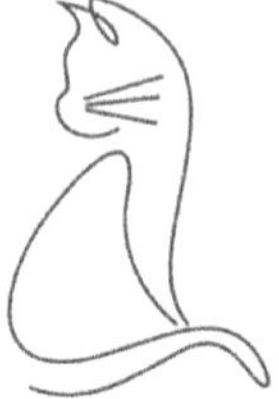

The first time I got a piece it was just like a dream
To do things I've seen on the TV screen

Then a loud scream had me humping like a rabbit
Found my first love and a man's worst habit

Pussy hooked me the first time I hit it
Addicted to the pleasure a fiend and I admit it
Tried hard to quit it

But that went fast, cuz everywhere I went I seen a nice round ass
And tight cheeks, I'm staring
Damn...I feel like a freak
The only thing I want to do is take her home to my sheets

Or on my bed spread I'm taking all my orders from the wrong
head
But I'll be going on a dive if she opens up those long legs

No time wasting, pure concentration
I swear I need to go to Pussy Rehabilitation
And every girl I'm chasing has got me in shit
So every little problem now I blame it on my dick

Invisible Chains

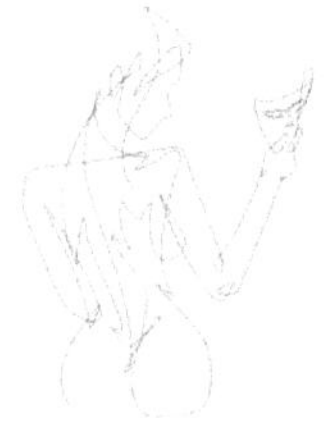

Hi there Alpha female, your beauty, strength and reputation
precede you
Who knows where this journey will lead to

I don't mean to intervene
But did I tell you how great you look in those jeans?

All those years in the gym and consistency have really paid off
And I really like the trade off
I'm inspired by your motivation as I bear witness to your dreams
of success
And now it's on the verge to finally take off

An when the whole world has it's handout
What do you do?
Keep to yourself? Try hard not to stand out..

Your drive is exhilarating
Your patience is liberating
But every now and then your neglect to my need of attention gets
irritating

But as long as there's respect and mutual understanding
The reciprocal attraction and satisfaction is enchanting as your
presence is demanding

I don't mean to flirt
But did I tell you how amazing you look in that skirt?

Sculpted legs with thighs to match that perfect bubble butt
That ripe peach swaying at the right pace as you strut

Your leadership, your mentality scares most men away
For they are not worthy as they fear they may ultimately become
your prey

Sometimes your independence can be your own curse
As you appear to be always in control, always so bold, always so
diverse

But every human being needs someone and some point to where
they can remove the mask, relax and wipe off the smirk
The only time you show vulnerability is when I'm penetrating you
deeply
You release the sweetest moans exhausted from your long hard
days of work...

Knocking at the wrong door

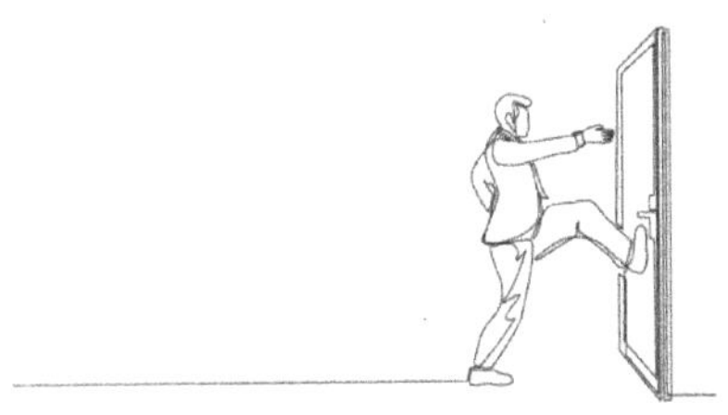

The forced interaction causes my brain to fraction
The response from her reaction
Clearly gave her no satisfaction

The blood clots, the mind rots
Until the temperature cannot be controlled
To where it becomes red hot, the have nots
yearn for the days of old

My response of being rejected
Makes me feel disrespected
Hard to hide my pride, my ego when my masculinity is being
tested,
Or maybe not tested, more like deflected or neglected
I've been here before, however not often so it's rare to be expected

I'd rather get in with my key than to break in
But then again when the fun and games are over it's all hard to
take in
Some say 90% of the thrill is in the chase
As the dog chases the cat, entitlement meets its demise in the face
of one sided lies at the end of the race

Sometimes being a stud isn't enough
Status, money and big dick may only get you a crush
Affection, patience and trust may never give you a rush
The wettest pussy in the world may never get you to hush

It's all bittersweet in the belly of the beasts
That has the taste for dark meat
Trying hard to be complete

So far I can't see, like crossing the sands of the Rub' al Khali
This woman, her pussy, her mind isn't mine
My key doesn't fit the lock of her design
So it wasn't meant to be

My House

When I come in the house I don't want to watch TV
I want to talk about you and me
The sun, moon and the stars

When I come in the house I don't want to sit on the couch
I want to talk about what we're all about
Neptune, Venus and Mars

When I look at you at times I wonder
Can I ever be satisfied?
Or am I forever caught up in being a hunter

Can I tell you my secrets?
Without you judging me even if they're not decent?
I sold you on the man you thought I was
But I somehow seem different as of recent

Am I too extreme for foolish things?
Abnormal to silliness and pettiness we don't need to address in all
the sorrow gossip brings

I've lost everyone I've ever loved
Am I cursed?
Destined to be alone sitting tall on my throne
Without anyone to share or converse
Well I guess it could be a lot worse...

I speak the universal language, both body and tongue
I kiss French, dance Latin, fuck Jamaican
For I am Superman, King Kong all rolled into one

So can I eat your pussy until you pass out?
Give you long hard dick all night long until you gas out?
Anything other than love or affection will surely be cast out?
No judgment only a few rules
Upon entry take off your shoes
And don't throw stones in a glass house

Baritone Pheromones

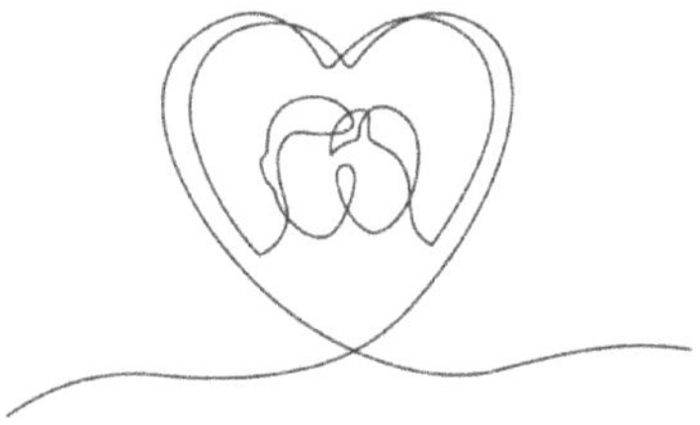

I walk in the scene with a gleam everyone's on their cell phones
Then all eyes on me as soon as they trace my pheromones
I deliver deep vibes like a baritone

Draped in the finest fabrics like James St. Patrick;
Ghosting on you bitches on my road to riches and bad habits

I have the power to seduce your girl without a single word then
take her back home
Send her back matter of fact after breaking her back bone...
Read that again with the exact tone

I'm the one, with whom she wants to bond, set the Oud Satin
Mood like Maison Francis Kurkdjian

The finest herbs the most exquisite hashish
Makes the beast spring from his leash
The Black Afgano, es me llamo, when I load my ammo
I proudly disturb the peace

I find solace in gray matters as black and white no longer suits me
Philosophical in my ways, until the rest of my days
But the dry down hits a spot of likeness to where you felt as if you
knew me

I'm a slayer, I'll be Killing them like I'm Kilian
Send her straight to heaven with my gold plated weapon
My fragrance, my scent
I am ... surely of the essence

Computer Luv

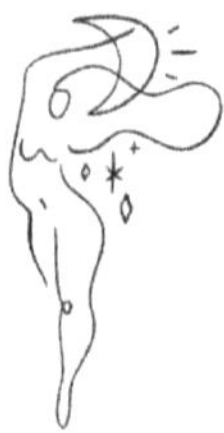

You know exactly what you're doing on that screen Ms. Thing
Those pants are way too extreme
Borderline obscene

But that's your M.O. to get all the attention
Display all your exhibitions
To get everyone hooked on your face, body and display
To feed the ego and drive the machine
And each "like" you get, is an extension of their true intentions

Am I any better? No not really
It would be naive and silly to not admit
From time to time your temptation gets the best of me especially
when I realize
Would I actually give a shit if I didn't have a dick?

So, I log in, your presentation never fails
Whether you're doing squats in the gym
Dressed up on your girls night out
Deliberately teasing us on film

For we are pawns in your little game
And when you're bored, you'll throw it all away and misbehave
Like a toddler seeking a new toy in order to feed the attention
crave

You call them fans, but they are more like slaves
Slaves of pleasure and desires, keyboard warriors fighting..
hopelessly depraved

To kiss your beautiful ass proudly self made as they flock
Commenting to be your fave, but never your babe, however, on
your worse day those that disobey may consequently get blocked]

If looks could kill and if sex was a weapon
You would be a 747 equipped with
hypersonic missiles ready to detonate in less than a second

In a sea of many fish you stand out like a great white
With all admirers at your mercy
Anticipating the next bite

Fisherman's Virtue

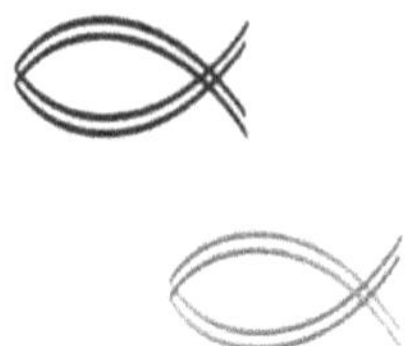

My boat is grand, the reputation is the greatest in all the land
Each fish that I caught in the past, I threw back into the sea or cast
away on the sand

My reputation precedes as I see you're not trying to go there with
me
Plus you don't have to respond
But let me ask, a year from now, what would the right one have
done, to leave you content on your decision, before the expedition
had even begun?

I may not tell you that you're beautiful every single day
Ahoy... attention is something which I'm always willing to pay
When it comes to you and only you I wipe my hooks clean and
extend my pole into the ravine to retrieve you anytime you get
away

I love the sport sailing the seven seas
With plenty of exotic fish nipping at my boat
With the ability to remain afloat
I power up to 67 turbine while other fisherman take note

Sometimes we crash but mostly we flow
Like a stream but in between there's a different salinity
Haloclines in the Pacific are different than Atlantic which
confuses the energy

I'm looking for a connection or a soulmate reflection
I'm looking for peace of mind and someone that understands
direction

Because if we're lost at sea will you come to my aid when we're both in need
Or watch us sink while other fish sabotage the boat if we concede

The Thrilla in Vanilla

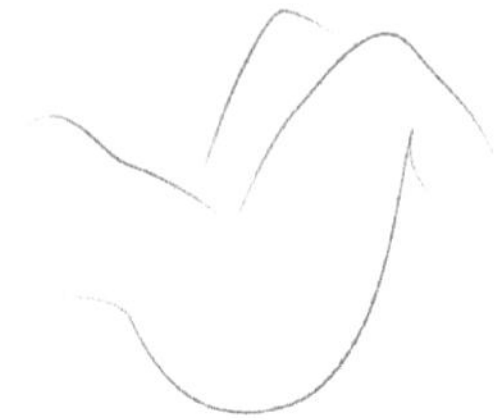

Secret lovers trying hard to be undercover
Ashamed of how the world views
Afraid of hidden colors
Exposed by new discovers
But the past seems to always revisit
And we don't want to relive it
We just want to be explicit
As long as no one suffers

Over 83 percent...
Confessed they would consent
To be or not be, which all seems content
To take a chance with that tall dark knight in whom she dreamt
Maybe it was meant
Or maybe even sent
Worst case she can repent
Yeah I can take a hint...

In public she gets amnesia
A symptom of jungle fever
But that liquid courage ignites a flame to where your curiosity
wants to dig deeper

Taking on a brand new world
Every woman and every man,
Every guy and every girl
Believers, achievers
Pleasurers and pleasers
French vanilla, butter pecan with a touch of mocha chocolate
blended up into a swirl…

The Night Shift

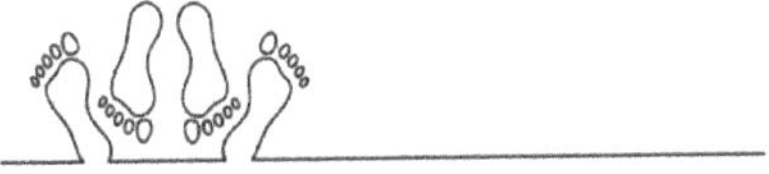

The clock strikes nine and I'm dressed to the nines
Later ... let's get together
Past times often end with bad times but then nothing lasts forever

Would you oblige if I stepped inside as soon as I get off
After stamping my time sheet, while you're dozed off to sleep
Quietly I creep as my next shift is about to start
I intend to fall deep into your trough

Urgency I felt, anticipating this very moment
Lonely...without you as the main component
The feeling is real, I seize it just as proudly as I own it

Like a thief in the night
Selfishly it's my job to steal your heart as you put up a fight
But I'm willing to work overtime to make things right

Though I'd rather be lusted than admired
I'd rather quit before getting fired
I'd rather not have any regrets be met before I'm too old and
retired

5:55 am

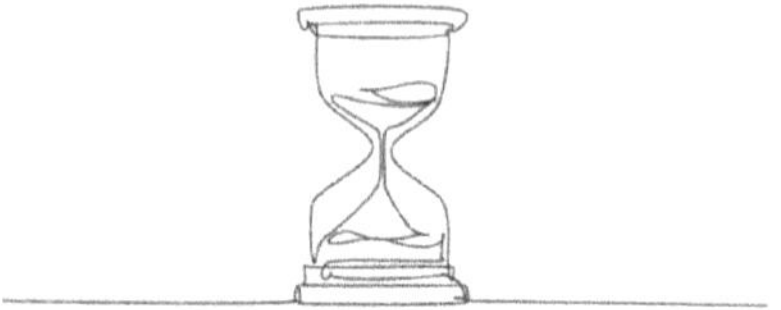

Right before the sun silhouettes
All the remorse and regrets
Fill up my amygdala with trivia
Of broken promises disturbed with interpretations of mutual
respect never being met

Ever dance with the devil by a pale moonlight
Ever waltz in the dark or salsa with a stranger, naive to any
danger
Until the moment hits you like a mushroom flight
Or when the cyclone emerges as a typhoon strike

Right before the sun, my emotions weigh a ton…

She loves me she loves me not
She lusts me she lusts me not
For the car to drive the engine has to thrive and start on the spot

Can you look a predator in its eye knowing that you're the mark?
Until it's time to be smart
Everybody plays the fool but you may be too good at playing the
part
Or maybe that's life imitating art
Though no one has truly ever broken my heart
For it was my own expectations that ripped it apart

She wants to lead the glamorous life without love, above all
things luxury brings
a world full of material girls and offspring from jaded and poorly
persuaded human beings

You don't need a reason
To change like the seasons
From Bodega to Venetian
Self reflection becomes an extinction like a Phoenician

She loves me she loves me not
She lusts me she lusts me not
A mental turn off is a physical burn off
Tick tock goes the clock
As time stands still when you're caught in the thrill...
Right before the sun my emotions weigh a ton…and for me that's
a lot

Zodiac Signs

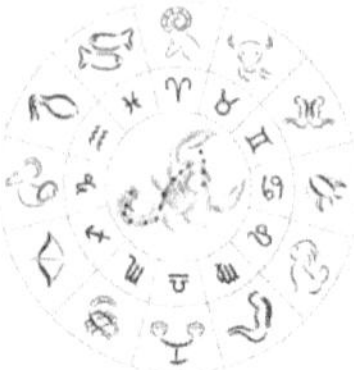

Sometimes the blind lead the blind
Then there are moments when we all need to unwind
When life seems unkind
Sometimes it takes a special type of man to bring out her divine
And if she gets out of line, it's fine
We'll just blame it on her zodiac sign...

Aries The first zodiac sign, she loves to be number one as she's one of a kind. Naturally fearless, bold and ambitious.

Aries both a lover and a fighter as she dives headfirst taking what she wants, she's direct and whenever she needs, can be vicious.

She represents the first lady, the alpha female.
Her beliefs, her confidence and her accomplishments reside in detail.

Taurus What sign exudes decadence? Indulged and fascinated with the earth and drawn to its beauty and elegance.

Taurus is the earth sign represented by the bull.
She is a celestial spirit, who enjoys both social and antisocial scenes, but her fixed earth quality has a trigger of stubbornness when provoked anytime she can pull.

Gemini Ever heard the expression two heads are better than one? Have you ever been so busy that you wished you could clone yourself just to get everything done?

That's Gemini in a nutshell.
Spontaneous, playful, and adorably erratic, Gemini is driven by
her insatiable curiosity embedded in her blood cells.

Cancer The crab weaves between the sea and shore representing
Cancer's ability to exist in both emotional and material realms.
Cancers are highly intuitive and their psychic abilities manifest in
ways other signs cannot comprehend and their sensitivity can
sometimes overwhelm.

The first water sign of the zodiac is willing to do whatever it takes
to protect herself and her family from attack.
She'll claw or crawl inside her shell habitat as an alternative way
to react.

To trust, live and love is what makes this Lunar Lady different
from all above.
The most sensual sign of the Zodiac the easiest to love,
Unforgettable, the one you're thinking of.

Leo Passionate, loyal, and infamously dramatic.
Leo is represented by the lion and these spirited fire signs, queen
of the celestial jungle evokes the ecstatic.

They're delighted to embrace their royal status; vivacious,
theatrical, and fiery,
Leos love to savor the spotlight and celebrate without inquiry.

Virgo Nit-picky, decisive and precise,
Virgos are logical, practical, and systematic in their approach to
life.

Virgo is an earth sign historically represented by the Maiden.
A deep rooted presence in the material world sometimes envied
by those who are hating.

She is a perfectionist at heart and isn't afraid to improve skills through diligent and consistent practice.
Seducing all that crosses her path, nose high to the sky like an Oscar winning actress.

Libra Balance, harmony, and justice define a Libra's energy.
As a cardinal air sign, Libra is obsessed with symmetry.

Social butterfly as she works the room with effortless epiphany.
Known to make friends rather than enemies.
Strives to create balance in all areas of life especially when it comes to matters of the heart that make the greatest memories.

Scorpio
Elusive and mysterious, Scorpio is one of the most misunderstood signs representing the eighth.
Scorpio, the second water sign that uses emotional energy as fuel, cultivating psychic and psychedelic wisdom evoking and embracing love, lust and hate.

The most sexual enigma, you can feel it when she enters the room.
Those piercing eyes "I desire" her confidence exudes as if she flew in on her broom.

Conflicted, esoteric but above all loyal.
Direct, revengeful and sometimes controlling if she's not treated as royal.

Sagittarius Ms. Always on the Go, this fire sign knows no bounds.
The archer woman is always on a quest for knowledge and running the town.

The last fire sign of the zodiac, Sagittarius explores her many pursuits

She craves a partner with adventurous attributes.
Always in route to conquer her next destination, she often plays by the rules that
only she chooses for she remains optimistic and sticks to her roots.

Capricorn The definition of Ms. Independent, Capricorn women are likely the ones that invent it,
From now until infinity she prefers to be ascendent.

Ruled by Saturn, hard work is not a factor.
Natural leader, stubborn at times but she's willing to sacrifice as she longs for security as she writes her own chapter.

Aquarius A Rebel with a cause...
Aquarius is actually the last air sign of the zodiac; her presence will cause you to pause.

Innovative, progressive, a defiant giant and revolutionary.
A natural born humanitarian, she doesn't conform to any stereotypes, her mood can
be warm as Spring but cold as January and February

Never to be told what to do,
Submissiveness is not her virtue.
A true fixed sign with a fixed mind.
Searching for someone that can make a promise and keep it, otherwise she may hurt you.

Pisces The most intuitive, sensitive, and empathetic sign of the entire zodiac, the last of the last.

As the final sign, the last of the three water designs; Pisces absorb every lesson,
the joys, the pain, the blessings
the hopes and the fears
learned by all of the other signs for infinite years.

Symbolized by two fish swimming in opposite directions.
Immersed in emotions as deep as the ocean they're able to cope in,
while searching for reflections and strong connections.

"I believe" is the motto and ambition in her power to achieve.
Draped in aquamarine, themed with elegant sheen, she yearns to
create her world in the eye she perceives.

TABLE OF IMAGES

All interior images were designed
by various artist from VectorStock.com

Poem Title	**Image Designer**	**Image #**
Mr. Temporary	AskhatGilyakhov	25613708
The Scorpio Man	AleksandrF	26086216
Esoteric Tongue	IlonaKitaeva	44275773
Tunisian Flower	knstart	32393606
She May Drive You Nuts	SyzSV	22610902
Pepper	ezgatin	2746728
What's for Breakfast?	OneLinePrint	37381673
Wandering Eyes	nine-0-nine	36529532
Lust Odyssey	Praiwun	42108657
Love Me Hate Me	BroStudio	23789059
Resistless	Artistock	22264737
The Big O	ExpressVectors	44252336
What League?	Valenty	21688673
Why Not?	gthd	35530970
Red Aura	dramaj	9542278
Primal Instincts	Valenty	44040168

Poem Title	Image Designer	Image #
Peaches and Cream	Nrsha	35049758
Can You Keep a Secret?	paranoid	31084147
Black Licorice	brankica	10568809
Forbidden Fruit	Remo_Designer	23851611
Principles of Economics	Praiwun	42108669
Sapiosexuals	Simple-Line	38022354
Hello Kitty	bellaxbudhong	43501607
Invisible Chains	JRMurray76	24219786
Knocking at the Wrong Door	Simple-Line	43573532
My House	pronick	42416865
Baritone Pheromones	pronick	42381948
Computer Luv	knstart	32393165
Fisherman's Virtue	vladwel	42934314
The Thrilla in Vanilla	Praiwun	43124780
The Night Shift	MarkRademaker	34019230
5:55 AM	Simple-Line	38022763

> *"We live in a world where everyone is perfect when pointing a finger but never when they look in the mirror."*
>
> Scorpio Man